WORDS FROM THE BIBLE ABOUT JOY

Be Happy

Edited and designed by Ben Alex

scandinavia

BE HAPPY
WORDS FROM THE BIBLE ABOUT JOY

Published by Scandinavia Publishing House 2012
Scandinavia Publishing House
Drejervej 15,3, DK-2400 Copenhagen, NV
Denmark
E-mail: info@scanpublishing.dk
Web: www.scanpublishing.dk

Concept, editing and design by Ben Alex
All quotes from New International Version unless otherwise noted
Photo copyright © Dreamstime pages 2,12,15,20,24,32,36,47,48,56,66,70,78,86,96,110,116,118
Photo copyright Janis Zroback pages 8,18,23,29,39,42,50,55,58,61,69,74,77,85,88,95,100,
103,108,113,121,122,127
Visit Janis at http://www.redbubble.com/people/paintability

Printed in China
ISBN 978 87 7132 045 9

Taste ye and see
that Jehovah is good.
O the happiness of the man
who trusteth in Him.

Psalm 34:8 YLT

Moreover,
when God gives
someone wealth and possessions,
and the ability to enjoy them,
to accept their lot and be
happy in their toil—
this is a gift of God.

Ecclesiastes 5:19

God gives joy

To the man who pleases him,
God gives wisdom, knowledge and happiness...

Ecclesiastes 2:26a

and happiness

You have given me greater joy
than those who have abundant harvests
of grain and new wine.

Psalm 4:7 NLT

Go, eat your bread with joy,
And drink your wine with a merry heart;
For God has already accepted your works.

Ecclesiastes 9:7 NKJV

I will be filled
with joy because of you.
I will sing praises to your name,
O Most High.

Psalm 9:2 NLT

Because of this
my heart rejoiced,
and my glory exulted;
also my flesh will dwell
in tranquility.

Psalm 16:9 ABPE

The Lord is my
strength and my shield;
my heart trusts in him,
and I am helped.
My heart leaps for joy
and I will give thanks
to him in song.

Psalm 28:7

I love the house
where you live, O Lord,
the place where your
glory dwells.

Psalm 26:8

You will show
me the way of life,
granting me the joy of
your presence and the pleasures
of living with you forever.

Psalm 16:11

O the happiness of
the nation whose God [is] Jehovah,
of the people He did choose,
for an inheritance to Him.

Psalms 33:12 YLT

They send forth
their little ones like the flock,
and their children skip about.

Job 21:11 NASB

The heavens declare
the glory of God;
the skies proclaim the work
of his hands.

Psalm 19:1

Lift up your heads,
oh gates, be lifted up,
oh Gates of eternity;
the King of glory
shall enter!

Psalm 24:7 ABPE

You will go out in joy
and be led forth in peace;
the mountains and hills will
burst into song before you,
and all the trees of the field
will clap their hands.

Isaiah 55:12

The Lord has made
his salvation known and
revealed his righteousness
to the nations.

Psalm 98:2

Let Israel rejoice
in their Maker;
let the people of Zion
be glad in their King.

Psalm 149:2

But let all those who
take refuge in you rejoice,
Let them always shout for joy,
because you defend them.
Let them also who love
your name be joyful in you.

Psalm 5:11 WEB

Let them praise his name
with dancing and make music
to him with tambourine
and harp.

Psalm 149:3

O Lord of Heaven's Armies,
what joy for those who
trust in you.

Psalm 84:12 NLT

Light shines on the godly,
and joy on those whose
hearts are right.

Psalm 97:11 NLT

The heavens
proclaim his righteousness,
and all the peoples see
his glory.

Psalm 97:6

It is good
to praise the Lord
and make music
to your name,
O Most High.

Psalm 92:1

He brought out
his people with rejoicing,
his chosen ones with
shouts of joy.

Psalm 105:43

There I will go
to the altar of God,
to God – the source of all my joy.
I will praise you with my harp,
O God, my God!

Psalm 43:4 NLT

...her saints will
ever sing for joy.

Psalm 132:16

Let the hearts of those
who seek the Lord rejoice.

Psalm 105:3

You have turned my
mourning into joyful dancing.
You have taken away my
clothes of mourning and
clothed me with joy,

Psalm 30:11 NLT

ng to dancing

The life of the godly
is full of light and joy.

Proverbs 13:9 NLT

The path of the righteous
is like the first gleam of dawn,
which shines ever brighter until
the full light of day.

Proverbs 4:18 NLT

Because
you are my help,
I sing in the shadow
of your wings.

Psalm 63:7

May the righteous be glad
and rejoice before God;
may they be happy and joyful.

Psalm 68:3

Worship the Lord with gladness;
come before him with joyful songs.

Psalm 100:2

Shout for joy, O heavens!
And rejoice, O earth!
Break forth into joyful shouting,
O mountains! For the Lord has
comforted His people, and will have
compassion on His afflicted.

Isaiah 49: 13

Rejoice in the Lord
and be glad, you righteous;
sing, all you who are
upright in heart!

Psalm 32:11

Restore to me
the joy of your salvation,
and grant me a willing spirit
to sustain me.

Psalm 51:12

When your words
came, I ate them;
they were my joy
and my heart's delight,
for I bear your name,
O Lord God Almighty.

Jeremiah 15:16

They will come and shout
for joy on the heights of Zion;
they will rejoice in the
bounty of the Lord.

Jeremiah 31:12a

I will rejoice in the Lord,
I will be joyful in God
my Savior.

Habakkuk 3:18

You make known
to me the path of life;
you will fill me with joy
in your presence,
with eternal pleasures
at your right hand.

Psalm 16:11

They feast on
the abundance of your house;
you give them drink from
your river of delights.

Psalm 36:8

Do not grieve,
for the joy of the Lord
is your strength.

Nehemiah 8:10

They will be like
a well-watered garden,
and they will sorrow
no more.

Jeremiah 31:12b

Rejoice in the Lord always.
I will say it again: Rejoice!
Let your gentleness be evident to all.
The Lord is near. Do not be anxious about anything,
but in everything, by prayer and petition,
with thanksgiving, present
your requests to God.

Philippians 4:4-6

And the peace of God,
which transcends all understanding,
will guard your hearts and your
minds in Christ Jesus.

Philippians 4:7

May my meditation
be pleasing to him,
as I rejoice in the Lord.

Psalm 104:34

With joy you will
draw water from the
wells of salvation.

Isaiah 12:3

So then, my brothers,
keep on rejoicing in the Lord.

Philippians 3:1a ISV

Indeed, you are
our glory and joy.

1 Thessalonians 2:20

But rejoice
that you participate
in the sufferings of Christ,
so that you may be overjoyed
when his glory is revealed.

1 Peter 4:13

Praise him with
tambourine and dancing,
praise him with the
strings and flute.

Psalm 150:4

...to bestow on them
a crown of beauty instead of ashes,
the oil of gladness instead of mourning,
and a garment of praise instead
of a spirit of despair.

Isaiah 61:3

Once more the humble
will rejoice in the Lord;
the needy will rejoice in
the Holy One of Israel.

Isaiah 29:19

I delight greatly in the Lord;
my soul rejoices in my God.
For he has clothed me with
garments of salvation and
arrayed me in a robe of righteousness,
as a bridegroom adorns
his head like a priest,
and as a bride adorns
herself with her jewels.

Isaiah 61:10

...rejoice that your names
are written in heaven.

Luke 10:20b

And we rejoice
in the hope of the glory
of God.

Romans 5:2b

Though you have
not seen him,
you love him;
and even though you
do not see him now,
you believe in him and
are filled with an
inexpressible and
glorious joy.

1 Peter 1:8

But the fruit of
the Spirit is love,
joy, peace...

Galatians 5:22a

To him who is able
to keep you from falling
and to present you before
his glorious presence without
fault and with great joy.

Jude 1:24

Rejoice greatly,
O Daughter of Zion!
Shout, Daughter of Jerusalem!
See, your king comes to you,
righteous and having salvation,
gentle and riding on a donkey,
on a colt, the foal of a donkey.

Zechariah 9:9

Let them praise
his name with dancing
and make music to him with
tambourine and harp.

Psalm 149:3

O the happiness of thy men,
O the happiness of thy servants...
these who are standing before thee continually,
who are hearing thy wisdom!

1 Kings 10:8 YLT

O the happiness
of all trusting in Him!

Psalms 2:12b YLT

O the happiness of that one,
who hath not walked in
the counsel of the wicked;
and in the way of sinners
hath not stood; and in the seat
of scorners hath not sat.

Psalms 1:1 YLT

I have told you these things
so that you will be filled with my joy.
Yes, your joy will overflow!

John 15:11 NLT

You have made known
to me the paths of life;
you will fill me with joy
in your presence.

Acts 2:28

n the Gospel

The kingdom of heaven
is like treasure hidden in a field.
When a man found it, he hid it again,
and then in his joy went and sold
all he had and bought that field.

Matthew 13:44

You welcomed the message
in the midst of severe suffering
with the joy given by
the Holy Spirit.

1 Thessalonians 1:6b

May the God of hope
fill you with all joy and peace
as you trust in him, so that you
may overflow with hope by
the power of the Holy Spirit.

Romans 15:13

Then they
worshiped him and
returned to Jerusalem
with great joy.

Luke 24:52

He makes me
lie down in green pastures,
he leads me beside quiet waters,
he restores my soul.

Psalm 23:1-2

71

His master replied,
"Well done, good and faithful servant!
You have been faithful with a few things;
I will put you in charge of many things.
Come and share your master's happiness!"

Matthew 25:21

But the angel said to them,
"Do not be afraid. I bring you good news
of great joy that will be for
all the people."

Luke 2:10

Until now you have
not asked for anything in my name.
Ask and you will receive, and
your joy will be complete.

John 16:24

I am coming to you now,
but I say these things
while I am still in the world,
so that they may have the full measure
of my joy within them.

John 17:13

Command those who are rich
in this present world not to put
their hope in wealth, which is so uncertain,
but to put their hope in God, who richly
provides us with everything
for our enjoyment.

1 Timothy 6:17 NLT

...so that by God's will
I may come to you with joy
and together with you
be refreshed.

Romans 15:32

He who has the bride
is the bridegroom; and
the bridegroom's friend
who stands by his side
and listens to him,
rejoices heartily on account
of the bridegroom's happiness.
Therefore this joy of mine
is now complete

John 3:29 WNT

His Lord said to him,
"Well done, good and faithful servant.
You have been faithful over a few things,
I will set you over many things.
Enter into the joy of your Lord."

Matthew 25:23

78

...even as David also doth speak
of the happiness of the man to whom
God doth reckon righteousness
apart from works...

Romans 4:6 YLT

I have a great deal to say to you all,
but will not write it with paper and ink.
Yet I hope to come to see you and speak face to face,
so that your happiness may be complete.

2 John: 1:12 WNT

And the disciples were filled
with joy and with the Holy Spirit.

Acts 13:52

O the happiness of him
whose transgression is forgiven,
whose sin is covered.

Psalms 32:1 YLT

And on that day
they offered great sacrifices,
rejoicing because God had
given them great joy.

Nehemiah 12:43

joy together

And why didn't you say
you wanted to leave?
I would have given you a farewell feast,
with singing and music, accompanied
by tambourines and harps.

Genesis 31:27 NLT

Then Miriam the prophetess,
Aaron's sister, took a tambourine in her hand,
and all the women followed her,
with tambourines and dancing.

Exodus 15:20

David and the whole house
of Israel were celebrating with
all their might before the Lord,
with songs and with harps,
lyres, tambourines, sistrums
and cymbals.

2 Samuel 6:5

In front are the singers,
after them the musicians;
with them are the maidens
playing tambourines.

Psalm 68:25

They rejoice in
your name all day long;
they exult in your
righteousness.

Psalm 89:16

You have enlarged the nation
and increased their joy;
they rejoice before you as
people rejoice at the harvest,
as men rejoice when dividing
the plunder.

Isaiah 9:3

Then maidens will
dance and be glad,
young men and old as well.
I will turn their mourning into gladness;
I will give them comfort and
joy instead of sorrow.

Jeremiah 31:13

...and the ransomed
of the Lord will return.
They will enter Zion with singing;
everlasting joy will crown their heads.
Gladness and joy will overtake them,
and sorrow and sighing
will flee away.

Isaiah 35:10

Then all the people
went away to eat and drink,
to send portions of food
and to celebrate with great joy,
because they now understood
the words that had been made
known to them.

Nehemiah 8:12

By the fruit of his lips,
a man enjoys good things.

Proverbs 13:2a

One who has
a cheerful heart enjoys
a continual feast.

Proverbs 15:15 WEB

Praise be to his
glorious name forever;
may the whole earth be
filled with his glory.
Amen and Amen.

Psalm 72:19

At that time Jesus said,
"I praise you, Father,
Lord of heaven and earth,
because you have hidden these things
from the wise and learned,
and revealed them to little children.
Yes, Father, for this was
your good pleasure."

Matthew 11: 25-26

For the earth
will be filled with
the knowledge of
the glory of the Lord
as the waters cover
the sea.

Habakkuk 2:14 ESV

My son,
give glory to the LORD,
the God of Israel,
and honor him.

Joshua 7:19a

95

Let them praise your
great and awesome name.

Psalm 99:3

May your deeds
be shown to your servants,
your splendor to their children.

Psalm 90:16

They will neither harm nor
destroy on all my holy mountain,
for the earth will be full of
the knowledge of the Lord
as the waters cover the sea.

Isaiah 11:9

For your Maker is your husband –
the Lord Almighty is his name –
the Holy One of Israel is your Redeemer;
he is called the God of all the earth.

Isaiah 54:5 NASB

..and I saw
the glory of the God of
Israel coming from the east.
His voice was like the roar of
rushing waters, and the land was
radiant with his glory.

Ezekiel 43:2

And they were
calling to one another:
"Holy, holy, holy is the Lord Almighty;
the whole earth is full
of his glory."

Isaiah 6:3

And the glory of
the Lord shall be revealed,
and all flesh shall see it together:
for the mouth of the Lord
has spoken it.

Isaiah 40:5 KJV

Every valley shall be raised up,
every mountain and hill made low;
the rough ground shall become level,
the rugged places a plain.

Isaiah 40:4

...then you will find
your joy in the Lord,
and I will cause you to ride
on the heights of the land
and to feast on the inheritance
of your father Jacob. The mouth
of the Lord has spoken.

Isaiah 58:14

In the last days, God says,
I will pour my Spirit on everyone.
Your sons and daughters will speak
what God has revealed. Your young men
will see visions. Your old men
will dream dreams.

Joel 2:28 GWT

Joy in the

And I will ask the Father,
and he will give you another Counselor
to be with you forever.

John 14:16

But the Counselor,
the Holy Spirit, whom
the Father will send in my name,
will teach you all things...

John 14:26

Exalted to the right hand of God,
he has received from the Father the promised
Holy Spirit and has poured out what
you now see and hear.

Acts 2:33

As they pass
through the Valley of Baca,
they make it a place of springs;
the autumn rains also cover
it with pools.

Psalm 84:6

He opened the rock,
and water gushed out;
like a river it flowed
in the desert.

Psalm 105:41

He changes deserts
into lakes and dry ground
into springs.

Psalm 107:35 GWT

And everybody will
see The Life of God.

Luke 3:6 ABPE

...till the Spirit is poured
upon us from on high,
and the desert becomes a fertile field,
and the fertile field seems
like a forest.

Isaiah 32:15

Begin the music,
strike the tambourine,
play the melodious
harp and lyre.

Psalm 81:2

As they make music they will sing,
"All my fountains are in you."

Psalm 87:7

All your robes are fragrant
with myrrh and aloes and cassia;
from palaces adorned with ivory
the music of the strings
makes you glad.

Psalm 45:8

For with you is
the fountain of life;
in your light we see light.

Psalm 36:9

Then the angel showed me
the river of the water of life,
as clear as crystal,
flowing from the throne of God
and of the Lamb.

Revelation 22:1

Jesus answered her,
"If you knew the gift of God
and who it is that asks you for a drink,
you would have asked him and he
would have given you
living water."

John 4:10

For the Lamb at
the center of the throne
will be their shepherd;
he will lead them to
springs of living water.
And God will wipe away
every tear from
their eyes."

Revelation 7:17

In the middle
of the garden
was the tree of life....
A river watering
the garden flowed
from Eden.

Genesis 2:9b-10a

There is a river
whose streams make
glad the city of God,
the holy place where the
Most High dwells.

Psalm 46:4

121

And if he finds it,
I tell you the truth,
he is happier about
that one sheep than about
the ninety-nine that did
not wander off.

Matthew 18:13

Rejoice with
those who rejoice;
mourn with those
who mourn.

Romans 12:15

Is any one of you in trouble?
He should pray. Is anyone happy?
Let him sing songs of praise.

James 5:13

Be happy, young man,
while you are young,
and let your heart give you joy
in the days of your youth.
Follow the ways of your heart
and whatever your eyes see,
but know that for all these things
God will bring you to judgment.
So then, banish anxiety from
your heart and cast off the
troubles of your body...

Eccleciastes 11:9-10a

But the fruit of the Spirit
is love, joy, peace, forbearance,
kindness, goodness, faithfulness,
gentleness and self-control.
Against such things there is no law.
Those who belong to Christ Jesus
have crucified the flesh with its
passions and desires. Since we live
by the Spirit, let us keep in
step with the Spirit.

Galatians 5:22-25

He who loves money
will never have enough
money to make him happy.
It is the same for the one
who loves to get many things.
This also is for nothing.

Eccleciastes 5:10 NLT

For he will not think
much about the years of his life,
because God keeps him
happy in his heart.

Eccleciastes 5:20 NLT